An OCD Exposure Coloring Book

Coloring Exposures for Sexual, Harming, Relationship, Religious, and Scrupulous Intrusive Thoughts

This coloring book is dedicated to the many individuals diagnosed with Obsessive Compulsive Disorder. This diagnosis is often misunderstood; the general population believing OCD is all about being 'clean and tidy.' I hope this is one more resource that corrects that misconception.

Obsessions can include a variety of debilitating and stressful themes including sexual, harming, relationship, religious, and scrupulous thoughts, to name a few. The recommended treatment, Exposure and Response Prevention, assists clients in exposing to and accepting these intrusive thoughts. This allows them to habituate to the anxiety that surrounds an obsession, ultimately recognizing that a 'thought is just a thought.'

This coloring book was developed with the intent to provide a creative way to expose to intrusive thoughts. Owning the coloring book is an exposure. Coloring the page is an exposure. Looking back at it is an exposure. Eventually you too will be able to see, hear, and say that triggering word or thought without the panic that accompanies it.

Amanda

The OCD Exposure Coloring Book

The OCD Exposure Coloring Book

The OCD Exposure Coloring Book

The OCD Exposure Coloring Book

The OCD Exposure Coloring Book

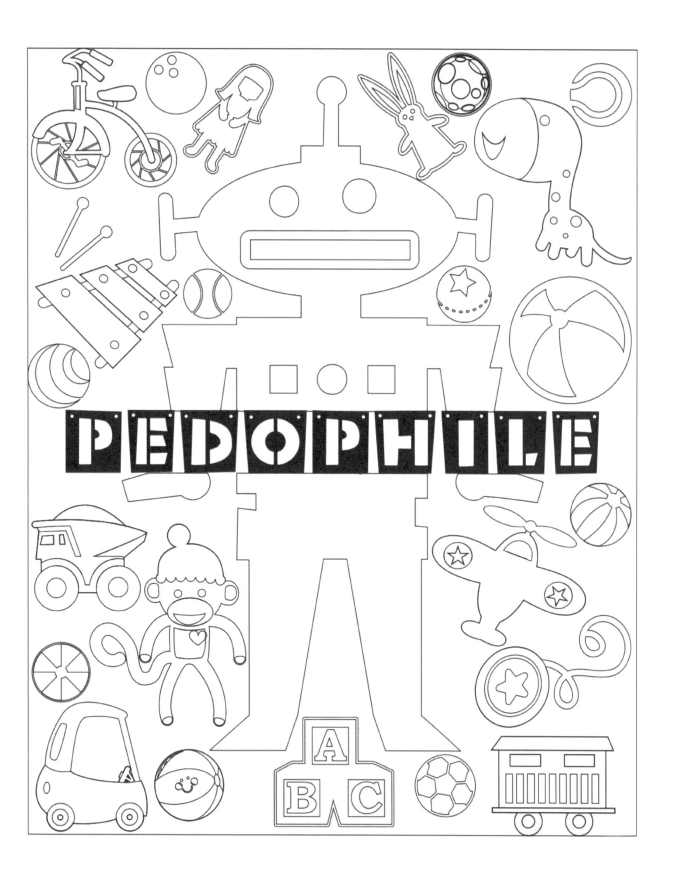

The OCD Exposure Coloring Book

The OCD Exposure Coloring Book

The OCD Exposure Coloring Book

The OCD Exposure Coloring Book

The OCD Exposure Coloring Book

The OCD Exposure Coloring Book

The OCD Exposure Coloring Book

UNCERTAINTY

The OCD Exposure Coloring Book

The OCD Exposure Coloring Book

The OCD Exposure Coloring Book

The OCD Exposure Coloring Book

The OCD Exposure Coloring Book

The OCD Exposure Coloring Book

The OCD Exposure Coloring Book

The OCD Exposure Coloring Book

Made in United States
Troutdale, OR
12/06/2023